180 Days

Reflections and Observations
of a Teacher

To Mel
for your friendship
support and being such
an inspiration
Stanley 3-27-2005

180 Days

Reflections and Observations of a Teacher

Stan Kusunoki

North Star Press of St. Cloud, Inc.
St. Cloud, Minnesota

Cover Design: Jay Monroe
Illustrations: Margarita Sikorskaia
Author photo: Claudia Hampston Daly

ISBN: 978-0-87839-790-7

First edition: March 2015

Printed in the United States of America.

Published by
North Star Press of St. Cloud, Inc.
P.O. Box 451
St. Cloud, MN 55320

northstarpress.com

Contents

PART ONE

OBSERVATIONS AND REFLECTIONS

PART TWO

APPLICATION—1

PART THREE

APPLICATION—2

PART FOUR

STUDENT WORK

Foreword

One day a couple of summers ago, while I was out and about, I ran into Stanley Kusunoki and his wife, Claudia Hampston Daly. As we have since we met back in 1996, we talked about our work: writing and teaching. But that day was different. That day, Stan mentioned that he was almost finished with a manuscript of what he called "teacher poems." The more he talked, the more excited I felt. Partly because he had been chronicling his years of teaching experience through poetry, but mostly because of the joy I saw on his face and heard in his voice when he talked about his students. Here is a man who truly loves his work and cares deeply about the children in his charge. He believes that all children, no matter their background, are small gems, worthy of being seen, heard and honored. In the opening poem, "Vessels," he says:

> Some are cut glass. They take the wine
> and shine, their own alchemy golden,
> reflects and glows on our faces
> Some are Libby glass, resilient, but plain
> they too sparkle as we open new vintages
> to keep them filled with wonder
> Even jam jars can catch light,
> hold our labors' offerings

I met Stan three years after I founded SASE: The Write Place, when my staff and I were seeking teaching artists for our school residency program. He had recently visited the class of one of my board members, and she enthusiastically introduced him. Over the next few years, he taught in residency programs for both SASE and The Loft Literary Center, and he eventually joined my board.

Stan has been writing poetry since high school but discovered his love of teaching through those residency experiences. He decided to return to school in his late forties and became a full-time teacher in 2000, after completing the University of St. Thomas's Collaborative Urban Educator (CUE) program. He has since taught high potential students, children in special education programs and second and third graders. He has also been a substitute teacher. For the last ten years, he has been teaching in the Shakopee public schools and was nominated for the Minnesota Teacher of the Year award in 2012.

180 Days: Reflections and Observations is a beautiful memoir in poetry, written at various times during Stan's sixteen years of teaching. The book is divided into sections: "Part One: Observations and Reflections" takes us from the children's elementary years through their high school graduations. Several of the poems in the early part of that section reflect on 9/11, juxtaposing that event with the everyday lives of his children. "Over a Decade" begins,

> . . . And yet every school year begins with an underlying dread
> security increased, eyes watchfull
> lock down drills now commonplace
> fear has become our *"e pluribus unum"*
> as once again we remember
> the one day in America
> that is everyday in Kabul
> in Damascus
> in Kandahar

In the next few stanzas, he recalls the morning of the 9/11 attacks, calling home for updates while the principal emailed parents. His strongest desire was to maintain calm and keep the horror that was happening out of his beloved classroom. The poem ends:

> And, I remember
> Kayla, and Jamilla and Nikki
> arguing for their turn on the swings

Dominique's laughter
as Raymond chases her
the second graders swirling
their whole world
this playground at recess

The final poem in that section finds him at a child's graduation.

So here I am a very confused bird
part mother hen
wanting to keep you close and safe
and part father eagle joyful
as I watch your wings
catch the updraft
You, all of you, spiraling higher and higher
to soar wherever your own winds
will take you

180 Days isn't just about being a classroom teacher. The poems in "Part Two: Application—1" were inspired by workshops given by fellow teaching artists at the annual Young Authors Conference at Bethel College in St. Paul. "Part Three: Application—2" includes poems he wrote to other teachers on special occasions.

"Part Four: Application—3" consists of poems written by his students, with the final poem, "Poem for Mr. K.," written by a student to honor him for her years as his student.

Every section in 180 Days: Reflections and Observations, indeed every poem, moved me deeply. Here is a book whose reflections on teaching is truly a work of art, one that should be read by teachers and parents, past, present and future.

Carolyn Holbrook
2015

PART ONE:

OBSERVATIONS AND REFLECTIONS

Vessels

They come to us empty vessels
It is our job to fill them with the pressings
of our feet and hands,
our sweat wrung from sheaves of paper
and blackboard scratching
The memory of those who worked this vineyard before us
Whose vintage we blend with our own
to pour into open brims

Some are cut glass. They take the wine
and shine, their own alchemy golden,
reflects and glows on our faces
Some are Libby glass, resilient, but plain
they too sparkle as we open new vintages
to keep them filled with wonder
Even jam jars can catch light,
hold our labors' offerings

Then, there are those like Jaime, Chantel
who have been dropped and tossed
and left in the alley. Each lesson
hemorrhages through kaleidoscope cracks and chips
we wonder that they hold anything at all.
And after ladle upon ladle rivulets across the floor
we understand only an eyedropper will do

And so by ladle or by drop, these vessels grow
while the glassblower waits for us to remember
that glassware can be reformed and made whole

Primary Level, 1

You learn quickly
It's all in the tone of voice
the difference between
tears and understanding
That jumping up and down
is not misbehavior
That asking how to spell "the"
is not a request for information

How a quiet turn of the head shouts
and echoes for days
You learn the importance
of tying shoes
of knowing the colors of the bus
though they are all orange
You understand quickly it is not your job
but their survival

Primary Level, 2

The Hmong boy writes in his journal
that I am his best teacher ever
because I let him do fun things

Fun? What is he talking about?
I, who more often than not
shoot Zeus's thunderbolts from my eyes
Pronounce doom and dread consequences

What fun is there in lining up over and over
sitting head down on the desk listening
and listening to the same sermon
not on the Mount of Olives, but on the plain
of the desk, the carpet unyielding?

What lurks outside these school walls
that makes this space a sanctuary?
Creates security in the chaos
of a first-year classroom—
comfort in the howling
of a first-year teacher?

Primary Level, 3

Claudia calls them my barnacles
these boys and girls who cling for dear life
who say "watch me!" on the swing
on the slide, arm over arm on the monkey bars
ask me to walk them home
to the cockroach kitchen and
laundry pile living room

Could you say to them,
"I'm no social worker"?
Could you turn away
"It's not my job"?
Could you hurry home
knowing their dinner's not waiting?

"What is the answer?" I ask the river
"Go with the flow," it splashes
"What is the answer?" I ask the sky
"Fly away fast," it breezes
"What is the answer?" I ask the Oak
"Grow thick bark" it gnarls
"What is the answer?" I ask the child
"Let me be a barnacle, just for now.
Let me be a barnacle till I swim by myself."

Cranes for the First Grade

This is a moment to savor and hold:
The end of the last day before winter holiday break
Kids lined up like Doughboy chrysalides
clutching shiny objects
Waiting for the bus line to shuffle forward

In this world of video games and "Reality" TV
Of Ritalin and foster care
Of news stories that read like B-movie plots
Of hungry stomachs,
bruises unexplained
They hold wonderment and awe

"He showed us how," they buzz
Their own mittened hands holding magic
that a hundred million store-bought toys
could not replace

The teacher sees their joy
against the darkness of the times
and marvels—How something small and simple
changes everything

11, September

The man on the TV says
"Everyone will remember
everything they have seen today . . ."
while behind him, over and over and over
we see the airplane angling
like a clipped winged gull
into the World Trade Center
see the billowing orange exhaling
the tower of steel and glass turned
into circus fire-breather
We wait for the bow, the applause
everything all better
and in growing horror sense
this is not an act—
the burp of flame
the roiling crumple
all real
and all real, the lives turned to ash

We are grown-ups
and cannot make sense of it
What do we tell them, these children of ours
now that America has been jolted
out of its two-century adolescence?
That its coming of age is any different
from theirs?
What do we say against the video images
to keep at bay the nightmare world
that seeps like smoke under classroom thresholds
How do we convince these kids
that life continues its raggedy path tomorrow—
that there is a constant
even when everything changes?

Mealy Worms

It is the third week of school
A week past the twin towers falling
like the wrong piece pulled
in a game of Jenga
and Jamilla is crying her eyes out
in the middle of the sharing space
The thick September light stirring
a dust halo around her, I reach to comfort
to give perspective
When she holds out her hand, I see it
curled like a fragment of French's fried onions
"My mealy worm is dead!"

My glib response freezes, my mouth, an "O"
choosing silence over instruction
This is her big picture
No transforming beetle her reward
for weeks of prodding eggs
daily feeding, but a husk
brittle and unfulfilled

My wish is for the mealy worm to live
Not just to dry the teary rivulets
on a young girl's face
but reincarnated, a silkworm
to spin a cocoon from the sunlight dust
around Jamilla and her classmates
That the darker dust, still swirling
in a swarm of cyclones
cannot shadow their world

Intermediate Level, 1

When I was in fourth grade
there wasn't any Ritalin and Allen
bit the teacher right on the breast
when she tried to take him to the principal's office
The janitor came in, and the principal came in
and it was the janitor's gray blur
and the principal's navy-blue blur
Mrs. Halvorson's tan blur
and Allen's many-colored stripes
careening around the room
creating a human kaleidoscope

It was better than a Disney movie until
Allen blew it by letting himself
get caught in a corner
Then it was all arms and legs waving
as the janitor and the principal
picked him up and carried him down
the hall, a legend in the making

Well, we have Ritalin now
but Allen's still around
cloned under assumed names
names he thinks will fool us
like Michaela, or Chou Seng, or Tyrone
It's still him, and if anything
the situation has gotten worse

Maybe dad's in jail, or just gone, period
or mom's working two or three jobs
and doesn't have time to make dinner
much less read a bedtime story

And maybe there's an older brother
who cooks crack, packs a piece
who will soon die right in front of everyone
as a gold-wheeled, low-rider Toyota
with a high-tail spoiler squeals away

Leaving us shaking our heads
looking at Allen in all of his guises
still just a kid with big, grown-up suitcases
clipped to his backpack
dragging him further and further behind
and us, not so much teachers as locksmiths
hoping to pick the combination
that will set him free

Intermediate Level, 2

You can see it in their poems
everything hits closer to home now
When I was in fifth grade, Kennedy was shot
They announced it over the school intercom
and we sat in our seats thinking something
was wrong with our ears. And then Gary and Patty
and I ran home because they let school out
to see for sure, on the television

Fifth graders here do not need the intercom, the TV,
the Internet, to tell them what's going down
They write about mom dying of cancer
of uncles getting shot
of brothers in prison
and they worry about the world tumbling
burying them alive—big picture asthma

Here poetry is more than an exercise
More than mere metaphor
It is clearing out the muck of everyday
It is opening the lungs to unsullied air
It is breathing
It is dreaming
It is flying to the place inside
the world cannot touch

Intermediate Level, 3

The sixth graders will call you an asshole
to your face—detention not a deterrent
They jump on each other because of a look
They fight over who won a game in Phy. Ed.

In Mr. Kriesel's sixth grade, I got into trouble
for pulling Sandy Swanson's ponytail
Now we find condoms at the end of hallways
Fret about who hangs with whom.

So it's a revelation for a substitute teacher
when folding origami cranes
transcends attitude and bullshit
that amidst the chaos, a couple
of lippy girls discover a zen moment—

The here and now of creases
the patience of molding golden paper
creating a third dimension out of two
A symbol of hope
The crane, yes, but more important
the smile that says "I can."

Intermediate Level, 4

His mind moves so quickly
all the teachers have trouble keeping up
frustrated when they demand to "see his work"
"It was just there," he looks blankly
"I see the numbers in my head"

The entire process of long multiplication
springing full blown, no baby steps
This fourth grader driving a Corvette
pedal to the metal on an Autobahn
of numbers and computation

And I wonder, following in my minivan
"How do you teach such a child?"
How to accelerate one already hurtling
at breathtaking speed
past curriculum guide rails?

Do we let him go
or slow him down to the point
where his internal GPS
can find the pathways
the circuitous route
seeing what he already knows?

Over a Decade . . .

. . . And yet every school year begins with an underlying dread
security increased, eyes watchful
lock down drills now commonplace
fear has become our *"e pluribus unum"*
as once again we remember
the one day in America
that is everyday in Kabul
in Damascus
in Kandahar

I remember a sunny day
the second graders at recess
their exuberance
an entire prairie in bloom
alive, alive
and how that kept me from crumpling
to the ground when Dan told
me and Julie and Tlotlisang
about a plane
and buildings falling

Yes, I remember the TV in the faculty lounge
remember the principal's e-mail
letters home to parents
calling home to get updates
because I didn't want the horror
live and repeated in the classroom
Yes, I do remember

And, I remember
Kayla, and Jamilla and Nikki
arguing for their turn on the swings
Dominique's laughter
as Raymond chases her
the second graders swirling
their whole world
this playground at recess

Subbing

The fifth graders are not fooled, not one bit
They hear the introduction, how pleased and excited
I am to be subbing (Good God!) at the end of the school year
In this class where not only the teacher, but the trusted student teacher
are nowhere to be seen, twenty-seven minds for once think alike:
"You are not, and never will be our teacher"

So we teeter-totter. The parking lot littered
with lesson plans discarded
as teacher and the students comprehend
it's not going to be done the same way
I struggle to learn all their names
they struggle to say mine

They pose me in the role of referee, trusted uncle, counselor, big brother
They find me a decent enough actor, so new roles emerge daily
And as each new script is played out
the class notches up one new connection
By the end of the week I swear I hear one kid say, "Hey teacher"

I am not fooled, not one bit
I am not the teacher who worked them through eight sweaty months
Not the student teacher either.
I am the blip at the end of their school year
Yet, a blip whose name they will pronounce correctly
Whose words and manners will stick like duct tape
stashed away from peer's prying eyes
in a secret place like used gum

Leavetaking

I knew long before I even stepped into the classroom
The hardest part is not the boy throwing chairs
The girl who won't sit down
Gabriella, who cries when it's math time
Or Frederico, who talks back when it's anytime

It's the letting go—arms empty
as these children go about unfolding their lives
Journaling their path each step a paragraph
And if we are lucky, a bit of us in the ink blots

I had not expected it to come so soon
The third week of a new school year
Names finally put to faces and voices
no warning, no good-bye hug

I am denied her quiet humor, giggly asides
a dramaturge in a class of bad actors
Monday morning, an empty desk
I do not move it aside

Classroom Vacant

I look at this cube
this container for learning
My thoughts bounce off bare walls
become colors, shapes, sounds
Childrens' footsteps, lesson plans
and stories fill the space

I listen for past echoes
the spirits of all who have taught here
wisdom gained from sullen girls
the boy whose father left town
the parents who worry about Eduardo,
or Mai-Leng, or Terry, or Lakeisha

I stop, wait, breathe it in
fill my lungs so that my exhaling
rich and full of possibilities
will spark the dreams of children
Young minds, like this classroom
ready for whatever comes next

Music Therapy

If only teaching could be a song then I would be a success
Look how hungry they are
They touch the guitar strings in awe
The magic of moving wire through air
of white nylon plectrum, nickel frets and wood

Hear the hunger in their voices
cascading voices for once in common purpose singing
over and over the same song
burrowing the words and melody
deep, deep into that safe place

I thought the learning would be in the lyrics
the message, the meaning,
the kids are reading
without thinking they are working at all

But in truth, it is a secondary lesson
to the voices, not quite on pitch
nor with perfect timing, still
coming together in song

Birds in the Mineshaft

They are still sensitive
can feel the danger adults
have long forgotten
And so we send them—canaries
or rock doves—newly fledged
into open mineshafts
to feel the upward drafts
that in adults' ungainly plummet
would be explosive

Should we wonder that after
two or more tosses into the darkness
they comprehend our intent
and feeling the power of their own wings
fly not downward, but up to open sky?

Long-Term

So here I am plunked like an immigrant
with immigrant fears
new faces all around
in front of me the unlit basement
what to do, what to say?
expecting at any moment, the INS agent
with the one-way ticket

finding instead
a new family of translators
and guides
of singers and dancers
of writers and poets
and a kettle always
warm on the hearth
a welcome not just for today
but for the long term.

Mattie's Jam

I open the jar of Mattie's jam and breathe in laughter
the students we shared those four months
songs at the end of Math: Maggie and Lorena both
wanting to sing solo the bridge to "Country Roads"

I open the jar of Mattie's jam and taste the moments
Joey's "high fives," Spencer and Seth—their silly sentences
magnetic on the tall black cabinet. Danny's M&M's
and scrawly drawings, all secret doors opening to treasures

I open the jar of Mattie's jam and spread it thick
Devonte's books and Padah's counting, the two of them
hiding in their own way behind doors, under tables
the racing wheelchairs—Shena and Cheenou

I open the jar of Mattie's jam and it spills over
on new blue counters rich with the fruit of many labors
of teachers' sweat and parents' wisdom
and children's voices, their expectant looks
as they dip their fingers in the jar to taste

Shakopee

Named after a Dakota chief
the remnants of the once vast prairie
ghost the hallways of this school
where the carpet still has that new smell
and the ceiling tiles are intact

The spirits wonder at the transformation
grassland to white man's outpost
to river town, now burgeoning toward
major school district status
They see the invisible needs
not broken faucets but learners' minds

How even in this progressive state
there is no mandate. No, it's left
to administrators, teachers and parents
who understand "No Child Left Behind"
is not a slogan for election time

It means all children served
not just the struggling,
not just those who get by,
but also those at the head of the line
for if those who lead lose interest, lose hope
then what can be expected of those who follow?

If We Do Not Believe the World Has Changed . . .

"Why did they do it?" asks a fourth grader,
"If they wanted to kill Americans they could have
just crashed into downtown or a mall
someplace where there are lots more people."

So begins a discussion of symbols, icons
Social Studies taking over Reading class
History superceding Writing

And I wonder if grown-ups along the Potomac
along the Tigris and Euphrates
at the headwaters of the Ganges, The Yellow River
The Volga and the Mekong . . .

. . . If any of them put this much thought behind their actions
what difference in the world?
How many more children still alive?

Ambassadors in Training, 1

"I don't get it," they say. "Why can't people just live together?"
The reading class reacts to new-found knowledge
that Judaism, Christianity and Islam share common roots
their heads swirl like dervishes coming to a conclusion
it's not faith, belief, spirituality, the driver
but greed and power
scarce water, scarce land, scarce and dwindling resources
it's not about "just folks," not about their lives

So what if fifth graders world-wide conferenced
Lacking the fear and prejudice of their parents
lacking the desire to impose their wills on others
seeing each other only as people
who listen to hip-hop
play video games
look skyward at Ursa Major and Polaris
and tell each other the names their cultures
give to the map of the stars

And what if this grand conference agreed
to move with the combined energy of ten-year-olds
to fix the mess before them
ideas building on ideas
a new quantum mechanics?

Could it be any worse than the peat bog
of finger-pointing and name calling?
behaviors we adults chastise
when it manifests in children
but dismiss when it's those we elect

Or could it be something better?
a new paradigm based on clean-slate
and unused stylus
on minds not yet sullied,
the minds of the fifth grade?

Ambassadors in Training, 2

"But," he says. There is always a "but" in these conversations
"Without war, there wouldn't be any inventions—we could be
like, back in the stone age."

There's a buzz, agreement, disagreement
and then a moment of nothing
everyone thinking of technology—even
household items, microwaves, radio,
everyday implements that spring
from the need to be one up on those across the border

"What about the Internet?" he continues, "computers
the gazillion aps . . ."

"Oh"
It hits
War is business
And since it is business,
there will always be someone
who wants to be a prophet
to make a profit
"But,"

Again, "but"
"If we weren't so worried
and scared, couldn't we think even better?
Couldn't we make even better inventions
if we all worked together?"

"Let's think about that," the teacher
recovers his voice
"A good place to stop
at least for today."

4, September

You think these are the same kids
Their appearance only slightly
altered over the summer
Spring leaves turned darker
harnessing sunlight
That is what you see
But deep inside
what feats of microscopic engineering
New roadways, the infrastructure
all redesigned for new traffic
that you will try to direct
Flowing, you hope, with few
traffic jams and fewer accidents
Humming with delight
at new shiny bridges and hard-
wired pavement the open
freeways of the start of school

And, heeeeere's . . .

. . . Gavin, the petulant boy with transition problems
who works by fits and starts
an engine in need of a tune-up
spark plugs, oil change—the whole package
looking at you, bright-eyed, "high five"

And when I say "You'll have to work
harder this year to get into my Math class"
He says, "I will, because I get smarter every year."

Oh, that we teachers could conjure
that transformation every year
in all of our kids!
How different the world would be
new visions before us that for now
remain invisible?

Drumming with the Fifth Graders

They complain about:

Drumming the background, repeated beats,
the canvas for words, for drum solos
More than the repeated strokes
"don, don, don, kara, kaka"

The concentration of really listening
really watching, everyone in synch
so they roll as one, take their turn
in the line without a dropped beat

The confining walls of quarter
and eighth notes, rests,
of fortissimo and piano
and keeping the beat, keeping
the beat, keeping the beat

I hear the complaints and smile
When parents and siblings and
next-door neighbors fill the chairs
they will sparkle like Roman candles
Drumsticks sprouting feathers
fledglings no longer, but Thunderbirds

High Potential

It is a strange sensation
Jumping off the deep end
but not yet touching the water
suspended like a bungee jumper
at the bottom of the ride
so tantalizingly close
spray on the face
but no immersion
not yet

I glance around, yes
there are others like me
face down, eyes full of anticipation
wondering will the water
be warm and welcoming
bracingly cool, or frigid and life sapping?
will we be carried by the current
into boulders and flotsam
run aground
or rise swimming like spawning Coho?

Teacher Work Day

The hallways are too quiet
Their occupation muted as
Teachers shuffle to their rooms
to each other's rooms for chatter
Some business in the workroom
A stray announcement floats on the air
It is not enough

The halls feel underemployed
They sulk a long sulk of clicking
keyboards and numbers
The shuffling of paper landfills
While teachers watch the clock, ruffle
through pockets for that elusive dime
needed with quarters
to deliver the godsend caffeine

The hallways stretch and sigh
trying to nap, smugly thinking
as the blind buzzers ring the day in
and the day out, "No one cares.
Not today, not today. Your yapping
useless as hall passes and lockers.
Save it for Monday when we all
have meaning once again."

Voyager Leaves the Solar System

"Arrgh!" papers crumple, pencils break
The fifth-grade math class has come to the border
trying to cross the frontier of the unknown
Familiar symbols now speak in foreign tongues
English words become Swahili
numerals transform into hieroglyphs

These students who have all the answers
who wave their hands wildly to be the chosen
the one who shows us how to do it on the board
now float their arms upward in frustration
brain synapses like solenoids not closing

You can almost hear that *"click, click, click"*
of engagement, then missed connection
engagement, missed connection
engagement, missed connection
reaching, reaching, to bridge the gap

Now I am the mechanic, the electrician
instead of the cheerleader on the sideline
Now I am the translator, the decoder
instead of the magician who pulls answers
like white rabbits out of their upturned hats

It's okay for me to enjoy this now
In a day, maybe two or three
the solenoids will slap shut-synapses
wired and pulsing with current
the hands again shooting up
"Pick me," "Pick me," "Pick me"

Immigrants

The new kids scope it out
transfers from another school
another district
look for commonalities
their eyes dart
to textbook covers they know
word charts with common meaning
They relax, just a bit when
hand claps and counting down
result in familiar behavior
when numbers follow the same algorithms
and the teacher calls on them
just like everyone else

And soon the teacher forgets
they are immigrants
integrated into this pond
that for now
is the shared ecosystem
where they are true citizens
adding their own biorhythms
to the mix

Graduation

My first cohort of students
who suffered with me
in that cramped
designed-to-be-an-office room
within the Media Center
is graduating
their high school class so large
the ceremony in a mega-church
instead of the High School gym

They file in their rows
not quite lock step
Some are panthers
cool and confident
Others chatter like sparrows
now fully fledged
at the feeder

Some test the waters
Junior college
time away
a part-time job
Others plunge
their courses firm
in their brave, new hearts

All of them explorers
Young Vespuccis
setting off in vessels
with sails, or motors
or the strength of their arms
for their own new world

Ch-ch-ch-Changes

Tough not to quote David Bowie
when queries for poems from students
now in Jr. High? No, High School!
return with texts
"Haven't written a poem for don't know how long
probably since your class."
The student laureate
now banging a hockey puck
bending a Fender "Stratocaster"
the writing diva now a volleyball star

You remember kneeling down for face-to-face
and now for some reason, crane your neck
to see them all new, some unrecognizable
some the same, but flashing drivers licenses

And even still, though you know they are not,
though there have been years and dozens of teachers
in between, it slips out
"These are my kids, my students"

Wings

The caps fly like a flock
of blackbirds startling off a field
of summer wheat
A pity
gravity pulls them to the ground
Will the reality of the times
do the same
to these young adults?
So wise in inexperience
Tested to tears
and so untested in the things that matter

In my dream they rise
like their caps, not blackbirds
but an exultation
of larks
that do not come to roost
Soaring with their imagination
until there is firm footing
and shelter
from the shifting climate

June 3

I didn't sleep so well last night
Perhaps I thought by staying awake
I could delay the sun's rising
Silly me! for here I am and here you are
our Janus time
looking backwards and ahead
and leave-taking
though really it isn't such a going away
bits of me go with you
or so I hope

And surely bits of you stay with me
helping me teach better
as I remember where you got stuck
The words you argued to have included
in the answers not in the book
But then, we seldom did things
"by the book" did we?
Your thoughtful and passionate debates
word play and play acting
now part of my instruction

So here I am a very confused bird
part mother hen
wanting to keep you close and safe
and part father eagle joyful
as I watch your wings
catch the updraft
You, all of you, spiraling higher and higher
to soar wherever your own winds
will take you

PART TWO:

APPLICATION—1

One of the great joys of my job is that I accompany fifteen fourth and fifth graders to the annual "Young Authors Conference (YAC)" at Bethel College in St. Paul. Before I was a classroom teacher, I was a "poet in the schools," and I am always curious to see what presenters will do for their one-hour workshops. It also gives me a chance to touch base with writing pals and mentors. The following poems are the "application" of just some of the many excellent sessions at the Conference.

Homecoming
from YAC 2013

Whenever I say, "Chicago"
I feel the wind pushing me down Wabash Avenue
under the "El," the pungent Chicago River
flowing backwards with my dreams

Whenever I say, "Chicago"
I taste sport peppers and celery salt
the sweet, neon green pickle relish
the sting of mustard, onions
the dripping slop of tomato
the garlic inhalation of Kosher pickle
all this topping a Vienna wiener
Hot dogs—the only way to make them—
a stone's throw from Lake Michigan

Whenever I say, "Chicago"
I hear the blues, not young "hot shots"
cramming too many notes into
four bar solos, like gulls at an open dump,
but "old man blues" slow like a bad dream
like a friend long gone, tomorrow never coming

Whenever I say, "Chicago"
I see a thousand mirrors
not like here, where I blend in
like soybeans in a wheat field
Whenever I say, "Chicago"
I'm gone

Subway Trains
from a workshop by Laura Salas, YAC 2012

Subway trains take you underground to cool places
Above ground trains are long and tedious
Subway trains move fast—they live in cities
Above ground trains live between cities

Subways go where they're supposed to
Above ground, cars and trucks and busses
have detours all spring and summer and fall
and then in winter, you're stuck behind snowplows
or big trucks flicking sand at you

Subways have cool people
playing blues or jazz on tenor sax
or some guy with a guitar
trying to be Dylan, or Springsteen
Where is the music at bus stops or taxi stands?

In subway tunnels you mostly don't see much
except amazing graffiti—how'd it get there?
Above ground, it's too much information
Dang, I wish I lived where there were subways

The Milk Bottle
from a workshop by Gita Gar, YAC 2006

Here I was such a big boy! The oldest,
the great example for brother, and cousins,
and countless generations to come
How I sucked in the air like a male grouse
when the sound of the milk truck
in the alley made me turn my head
like a dog hearing the Milk Bone box rattle

I could imagine
How proud mom would be that I—
All by myself—
brought in that heavy milk bottle
How she would pat my head cooing
"My! What a fine young man you are
helping me so much around the house!"
Her smile sparkling as she wrapped me
in a hug like a blanket, the warmth
of all the mamas in the world
And in that moment, I never imagined
the milk jug slipping . . .

Old Bogie Boogie
from a workshop by Mai Neng Moua, YAC 2006

Someday, I will be an old man shuffling with sandpaper feet
and raisin skin, but I will still rock 'n' roll

I will still rock 'n' roll with a guitar for every mood
One that sobbed for the blues, a slinky one for jazzy times
One in muted colors for whispered memories after midnight
And one gangly, spangly, glittery loud and crunchy
for exuberant hymns and tirades, but I will still teach

I will still teach with seeds in hand, the Midwest Prairie
in the south of France, or in Hawaii, skillet and spatula
raised to show the perfect tuna risotto
In Japan, I will teach rock 'n' roll
on samisens and taiko drums, but I will still write poems

I will still write poems that make students sit up and sing
Their songs carrier pigeons to places they can only imagine
while grown-ups reach far, far down into their mind's mine
uncovering childhood gold they had forgotten
Poems that make Tyrannosauruses
in corner offices weep and repent, but I will still have my van

I will still have my van, but it will be the perfect spaceship
to carry me to all these someday places and
all these someday dreams will fit into the back of it
Suitcases packed overflowing for the journey
with the music turned up really loud

Yellow Raft Smiling
from a workshop by Diego Vasquez, YAC 2006

1.
I am in the south of France
along the Mediterranean Sea
it is balmy and calm—a Zen meditation
I am walking along a coral beach wondering
why I have never heard of coral in the Mediterranean
When, near a blue railing I see
a yellow raft smiling
a green and purple grin
It says, "Take me out to the ocean."
Why not?

2.
Yellow Raft, smiling says
"Put down your axe
We don't do things that way
Not here in these woods
of old stand White Pine."
I am not sure if I am in danger
or if he is just giving me a friendly
warning, startling me as he did
seemingly sprung from the tufts
of pine needles drifting
the forest floor
His eyes are fair weather
but there is lightning in the pupils
so I comply, put down my axe

I ask in a voice like dry leaves
in November, "How do you do it then?"

"That is not for me to tell,"
he answers in a thunder crack
"Sit here tonight and tomorrow night
and the night following
Take the water that falls
from the canopy for sustenance
and move only with your eyes."

Let the School Year End
from a workshop by John Minczeski, YAC 2005

Let the school year come to an end!
Not like the slow train leaving in the night
its whistle long and mournful
Not like the tired second hands
on the clock in the cafeteria
Not like the driver of the tan Volvo
in the left-hand lane
going fifteen miles under the speed limit
Not like the lazy odor of charcoal
in Jean and Joan's grill
getting brats ready for the weekend
Not like the sap running
in the Maple where Jamison
is patiently hammering a tap
sugaring bucket by his muddy boots
Not like the steely waiting room
where kids with strep cough at you
forgetting the elbow rule
Not seeing the box of Kleenex
on the receptionist's desk

But . . .
Like students in the back of a bus
on a field-trip, Taylor and Marissa
hand-jiving sing-song
But . . .
Like the big roller coaster at Valley Fair
poised for that last big dive downhill
But . . .
Like a conga line in a crowded hall

hands raised in the air
full of expectation for
what happens next
Yes! Let the school year come to an end!

PART THREE:

APPLICATION—2

It was not intended to happen—I wrote a poem for a teacher friend who was having a baby, and she read it out loud to the staff at her baby shower—a new tradition! Since then, events in the lives of the staff at my school carry the expectation of a poem.

So a sampling of a different application of "teacher poems."

The Hole in the Day

There is a hole in the day that no one can fit through
Except the one who has just gone
It shimmers a vague emptiness
Without meaning it seems
Until we approach it and peek through
See all the memories it holds
All the days are there to visit
All the laughter and wisdom heard again
And if we pay close attention
A touch, a scent

There is a hole in the day that no one can fit through
But visit long and often
This wellspring in the middle of the air
Understanding that this place
Shimmering
Is no longer empty and meaningless
But the place where a soul still lives

Confluence
For J., 6-1-2012

We begin as mountain rivulets
Tumbling and jumping from the spring
Sometimes mingling
Sometimes falling apart
Some even trickle away
But those who make it to the forest floor
Grow stronger
Become streams

How wonderful then when two rivers meet
Strong in history
Filled with memories to share
The stream, even the rivulet
Still there but deeper
The current stronger
As two flow into one
For the long journey
To the ocean

Belated?
For S., November 9, 2012

The poem is late for the wedding
A day that's here and gone
Remembered in stories and photos
And anniversary dinners
gifts of paper, wood, iron and gold
A day
A time
A place

But these words are not late at all
For the marriage
Unconfined by clocks and gowns
Beyond the anthems
The altar
The attendants
Beyond time itself

The poem is not worried about missing
A date
For it has eternity to celebrate

Mixed Metaphors
for Mr. T., 3-2-2012

I had all these metaphors
Music making and marching to new drums
And harmony and improvising off the score
But it wasn't going anywhere fast

But what a new man you will be
some physical changes perhaps but,
Oh, the experiences you will have!
The new skills you will learn
the frustrations
And moments of unspeakable
Full brass fanfare
As you welcome this baby
You have had a part in making
while making yourself over
With each new change in the score

Play It Forward
for M.O. on her retirement

It's not like I am really saying good-bye
Yes, I will miss the theater talks
And movie recommendations
Chats in the hallway
But you will be here
As your students come my way
The foundation you have laid
Played forward in ways
None of us can imagine
What spark of you will illuminate
a fouth grade math lesson
Propel a fifth grade discussion
Grace a third grade story?
Even at our best
We only pick up what our predecessors
Have given
And you for so many years
And for so many students
The bedrock
So you know I will look forward to you
every day
for years to come
In the questing eyes
The eager raised-up hands
The confident stride
Your students, now mine
who know
They have started
on firm ground

Pathways
Congrats to N.

You have been making your own pathway
Watching your step
Skirting around briars and thorns as best you can
clearing the underbrush as you go
Sometimes a scrape
Sometimes rain
sometimes full of sunshine
But solitary

Now another path has joined yours
Another pair of hands to make the pathway
less rough, clearing the thorns
Quicker work
So that the journey
Is not so much a task
As an adventure

Interdependence Day
for K. 5-11-2012

In July, we will be celebrating Independence Day
While you will celebrate something else
Interdependence Day—as you bring
A brand new life into this world
Needing you for everything

And while we watch the fireworks
You will have your own
From the birthing, to the first cry
To the tiny body
against your shoulder

And while the fireworks we see fade to smoke
You will have them every day
From the first bottle
To the first step, to first word
A continuing celebration
Of your new state
Of interdependence

Spring Concert
for B., 4-20-2012

First it was a solo
Single notes on one string
Then a duet
Two strings in harmony
Then three strings
with chords
and triplets and arpeggios
Now another voice is added to the mix
A full concerto
for the finely tuned strings
of your family

GPS
for D.C. May 23, 2013 On your retirement

As a first-year teacher in Shakopee
a new district
a new position
new curriculum
Not much of a road map
How to get where I needed to be?

Who knows how much sleep I would have saved
had I known in advance
That there was a personal GPS
Ready, not only to show the roads
But where the detours were
The speed bumps and the potholes
The places where the pavement was not so firm

So that ten years into this adventure
Nearly a thousand students
have had a better teacher
Because of Mr. Cate's persistent calm
and fiery wisdom
They all take a bit of him with them
On their own brave new roads
Not lost, but searching
The gift passed along

PART FOUR:

STUDENT WORK

What is a book of teacher poems without the work of the students? It is a tradition among Japanese writers to include the work of their proteges, so here are poems by students—some written while they were with me for the Young Authors Conference, some written as secondary school students.

The Scratch at the Door
by Alyssa Voit, 10-22, 2013

Tiny paws scratch the door
A small "Mew"
A curious daughter tiptoes around the corner
Scrawny thin legs and a shaking, dripping body
Full moon eyes beg for warmth, for food
Deep rumbles slice the windy night
As the small creature is lifted and cradled
Given a warm saucer of milk
And a dry toasty place to rest for the night
And soon the small kitten is next to the fireplace
Being cuddled by the girl
Warmth embedded in between them
Love filling the air
A gold mist
Circling them
Protecting them like a fierce lion
No harm, no worries
Just love

Booklin
by Emily Graba, April 3, 2012

My poetry takes me . . .
To many amazing places
But my favorite place of all
Is Booklin, the land of books

It's kind of like a library
Except with no shelves
And books larger than men.
There are sofas and beanbags
And in the center of the room
There is a fireplace
Where everyone can gather and tell stories

Here, your senses are more alive
You can smell the hot cocoa
And the wood fire burning
You can see the words on the page
Feel the pages turning
You can taste the hot cocoa
And the smoke in the air

You can feel the warmth
The fire, the blankets, the hot cocoa

Anyone who loves to read
Can come here and enjoy
The peace and quiet
Here, everything is magical
No one has to do anything
But read on and on

And nothing can bother them
Pesky little brothers or barking dogs
This place is all I need
The peace, the quiet
Everything is perfect

Where My Words Take Me
by Mihika Sathe, 4-06-2010

My words, Like "please and thank you"
Can take me to gratitude
Where everyone appreciates each other
Like a sea of gratefulness
My words flow freely like little white doves

But some should not be said
Like things that can hurt people's feelings
and discard them as a friend
Mean words can make an impact
Like thunder hitting someone's heart
I can taste the bitterness
And hear the heavens shouting
I can see that my words were hurtful
I can feel my muscles tightening

Kind words that are spoken
From a good heart
Are like masterpieces of art
They can bring joy and happiness

I wonder how the world
Without any words would be
It would be like a day
Without the sun
Shining on me

Where I'm From
by Gabriela Leovan, 2013

I am a believer
Swimming in an ocean where things are not always clear
Molding my life like the clouds—
The mighty shape-shifters of the sky
Who knows what adventures await
I am from the crackling blaze, alive and dangerous
Whispering forgotten secrets in a language no one knows
I am an entrancing creature
Burning high with orange and red highlights
Maybe blue, green or purple
Luminous

I am of my spunky mystery terrier
Dangerous hunter and lovable brat
Grounding me to the couch while I read
Snoozing the day away,
Her fluffy white chest rising and falling

I am from my mother
Loving, caring, supporting
She is the beacon and I the boat
She is the port, in which I was built,
From which I would leave on my maiden voyage

Who is from swimming?—I AM!
I slide through the water manipulating the currents to my desire
I once was an elephant in the water splashing, slipping, and drowning
Now I am a new aquatic creature in my own right
Born to make water look like a joke

I am from reading
Sparking my imagination in a swarm of fireflies
Drinking from the fountain of knowledge
Tingling anticipation as I turn page after page
Reveling in this woven tapestry, following each thread
As hours fly by
Until I wake up again, again, and again

Black
By Gabriella Leovan, 2013

I've never understood why people like white
White is nothing, the color of absence
Black, now, black is there
It fills and muffles the silence
Holds us together like invisible ropes
Yet it's filled with misunderstanding
It calls for the bigger picture
Black does not care about details
But people fill in their own details
Causing misunderstanding and fear
They fill the black with imaginary monsters
While the real monsters are in the light
Laughing
Black is misunderstood, the color of misunderstanding
That's probably why it is the color of death
Death is the ultimate misunderstanding
Black is like most humans, it's misunderstood
But black is still there hugging everybody, no matter how much they fear it
It covers you with an invisible blanket
And many think it is the light that does it
But black finds a way through the light
As your shadow
Black never leaves you

Fiction Revolution
by Hannah Becraft, 10-22-2013

Moonlight reveals another way
For light is not gone
Nor is it ever
And the moon has set
Get on the sun chariot
And ride it to the land of imagination
Now when the sun is setting follow the moonlit path back
For on the darkest night, there is beauty
A sense of mystery
Enchantment
Actual state of reality

Reality isn't people telling what is and isn't real
Reality is you
Believing whatever your heart desires
Believing in dreams
Believing what you imagine
Being you

Be that one silver feather
On the night raven's wing
When you are shed
Travel by wind
Fall to the ground
And grow
Grow tall, grow strong
Grow UNBREAKABLE

For a poem isn't as simple
As a piece of writing
It's a piece of a prophecy

In the story of your life
It's a piece of a song
Left unfinished in the dawn
It's a piece of the notes
Written on your heart and soul
It's a PART of a REVOLUTION
And YOU are part of the GENERATION
So write
No one can hold the pen
So draw
No one can say no
So believe
No one can tell you, you're wrong
So dream
Because fiction is stirring in the realm where it sleeps
So IMAGINGE
Because the world
Is changing
Because the revolution
Brought fiction to life
Allowed us to dream
To believe
To IMAGINE
Because imagination,
Is the only weapon,
In the war against reality
WE can make fiction real
WE can spread joy
WE CAN paint the world,
The colors of happiness
WE can live in fiction
BE the GENERATION
That CAUSED the REVOLUTION.

Untitled
by Joely Kelzer, 2013

The smell of lake water fills my nose,
The rocky dirt crunches against my toes.
Trees stand guard, towering above the cabin
Down by the lake the loons coo.
The waves crash, excited against the shore
They ripple and glisten and sparkle even more.
The sun shimmers off the water and hugs the soft grass
And the wooden dock rocks back and forth.
The campfire crackles, the dog sits and howls
My feet slide into the water
Slimy scales graze against my toes
I jump—I shriek in surprise
as the fish flops out of the water.
After all the ruckus it soon goes back to "normal"
Time and time again, there are fish flops and big waves disturbing
the calm
But you see true happiness cannot be held in the palm
There are waves, bumps and rocks
But the beauty of the lake stays
There are splashes and clashes
But your smile never fades
For when you're on the lake, you're lucky enough

The Game to Catch Game
by Snigdha Panda, February 19, 2013

Greenery and shrubs engulf him,
The pierce of whistling wind reverberates in his ears.
The crackle of autumn leaves,
Looking like old parchment.
Silence.
The game is simple—
Hunter versus the prey.
Hiding behind a fallen tree
Old glass-eye looks searchingly,
The hunter nocks his bow,
Fitting an arrow perfectly into the groove.
Lines up with that of "glass-eye,"
Holds his beath
Lets the arrow fly,
And the breath flies with it.
The breath of death,
It hits the deer with amazing accuracy.
And so—such a game ends.
The game to catch game.

Untitled
by Phoebe Hessen, 2013

tired cerulean nails,
crumpled Sunday afternoon
and there are clocks everywhere
time peeks around evasively
struts on toward the bus stop
a briefcase full of innocence
in its crooked grasp
crimson voices call warnings
but this battle was lost before it began
while thieves disguised as walls and watches
saw you collapse into tomorrow
too late to be saved
too stubborn to regret it.

Society's Standards for Measurement
by Phoebe Hessen, 2013

this isn't a poem about society.
or measuring.
It's about sidewalk chalk on a dirty inner-city street
and waking up smiling on to a gray dawn after a night filled
with stars.
pristine lakes so cold they strip you of breath,
keys without locks, unexpected music
and the smell of Christmas that you can't quite remember
in the spring.
it's about that feeling—
back-to-back with the ruler
two feet on the scale
all eyes on you.
you're not sure how you're supposed to be
you just know what you aren't.
Its about you and what I know you are.
you are that dog-eared page of a second-graders favorite book
the sun off the hood of a rusty white car
a bird feather in freefall, sixty-seven cents
left on a sticky restaurant table
and the answer to a question no one asked.
It takes an artist,
or at least an individual,
 to measure the beauty of
painted fingernails bitten to the quick
and lipstick kisses on yesterday's coffee mug
but they hold the balances
and the gold stars

Poem for Mr. K.
by Cecilia Lovinger

Seasons change and time goes by
Our old group leaves the nest
All derived from a common place
HP was the best

Math geeks and athletes
Our own breakfast club
All so different, yet so alike
We came together without great strife

Passing now in the High School halls
An everyday routine
New cliques have been formed
Out of the storm we used to be

The unbreakable bond of our old classmates
There will always be a trace
Inside we all remember our discussions and our past
Some may not show it, but it's always there
The memories from that class

Something all shared by us,
No one else can possess
A melting pot of personalities
Of which truly I was blessed

To be a part of such a crew
An opportunity of a lifetime
A club I will never forget
The intellect—sublime

Becoming a member of this family you can't forget
Large brains squished into a tiny room
I will never have regrets

Still to this day we get together
Remembering the songs we sang, the material we learned, the laughter shared
With friends we'll have forever

Acknowledgements

"Primary Level, 1" appeared in *Artword Quarterly*, Number 22, Fall 2000, as "Primary Level."

"Vessels" was origially published in the program for the celebration of the Collaborative Urban Educator (CUE) alternative licensure project, Cohort 9, June 2000.

It is dangerous to start listing names when thanking people who were pivotal in bringing this first book of poems to life. Carolyn Holbrook and Mary Jo Thompson have been pushers and supporters since the beginning of my adult life as a poet, but are significant for this book: Carolyn was the one who challenged me to get a manuscript to North Star Press, and as director of SASE: The Write Place, got me to jump in the deep end of this great community of writers. Mary Jo was the impetus for me moving from "a poet in the schools" to a teacher who is also a poet: First as a workshop partner, then as a coordinator for teaching artists at the Perpich Center for Arts in Education, and finally, the kick that got me to go for the CUE project, and the profession of teaching.

If it takes a village to raise a child, it takes a state to raise a poet. Thanks to staff and former staff at The Loft, including Mary Cummings, Deidre Pope, Vanessa Fuentes, Jerod Santek and Bao Phi; Sandy Augustin for her enthusiasm as Director of Intermedia Arts; David Mura, mentor and "soul brother;" Evelina Chao, mentor for the Loft's "Asian Inroads" mentorship; workship partner John Coy; Barbara Cox and all the staff and teacher-artists at the Perpich Center for Arts in Education; Lia Rivamonte; Carol Connolly and her reading series at the University of Club; the Reverend Alla Bozarth for wisdom and clarity (and a marriage!); Jeanne Mortinson, Trudi Taylor, and Leah Lewis-Frazier at the University of St. Thomas CUE project; and all the staff at Dayton's

Bluff, Four Seasons and Expo schools in St. Paul, and Red Oak Elementary School in Shakopee.

In memoriam, for Zelma Wiley, mentor for the St. Paul cohort of CUE-9.

Special thanks to Nancy Katzmarek and Mitch Perrine—principals who understand where I'm coming from, and provided/still provide the guidance to be the teacher I am.

Of course, teaching doesn't happen without students, so to students past, present and future: You're the reason for this book!

Claudia Daly is not only my wife and best pal, but top-shelf editor, project manager, counselor and therapist. I am one lucky merganser!